How To Change Your Way Of Thinking
by Andreas Michaelides

How to change your way of thinking
ISBN: 978-9963-277-07-0
Cyprus Library.
www.cypruslibrary.gov.cy

I dedicate this book to a genius that unfortunately is not with us anymore.

"I take this scientific attitude, that everything you learned is just provisional, that it's always open to recantation or refutation or questioning, and I think the same applies to society."

Aaron Swartz

Table of Contents

Find more about me and my
books at my webpage
www.thirsty4health.com

About the Author

Andreas was born in Athens, the city that gave birth to Democracy, in Greece, the country that taught to the world how to live, think, and have fun. He grew up in the beautiful island of Cyprus.

With both of his parents bibliophiles (and his father a high school teacher), Andreas grew up with a love and appreciation for literature. In addition to the books he borrowed from the school library, a stack of encyclopedias taught him about the world. A history lover from age 13, he devoured the memoirs of Winston Churchill and Charles de Gaul, and by age 17, he had read all of Julius Vern's books.

After serving his country for 26 months immediately after finishing high school, Andreas studied in Patra, Greece to become a computer engineer. With his Master of Computer Engineering and Informatics, he began working in the Informatics Department of the local university hospital, and started reading again with a vengeance.

In 2004, Andreas authored his first book, a historical novel that has not yet seen the light of publication. Leaving it unpublished made him feel like a failure, but a lot has changed since then. Eleven years later, he has successfully quit smoking and has been smoke-free for the past six years. He has also started running again and managed to lose 26 kg (57 lbs).

Andreas has run three marathons, as well as many half-marathons and other shorter races. His love for running is what renewed him and actually saved his life.

Multiple medical problems pushed Andreas to research and experiment with a plant-based diet; since 2013 he is following a whole plant based diet.

In addition to running, Andreas enjoys hiking, cycling, playing basketball, camping, photography, and going out with friends and family and having a good time.

Attitude changes

I am at a point in my life where I can say with a large amount of certainty that I am very satisfied with myself. Well, with the exception of my very recent divorce, all aspects of my life are going where I want them to go. I feel more mature, and I don't get angry and upset as I used to be when I was younger.

My patience increased dramatically, I am more understanding with how other people behave in general, or how other people behave towards me and my family.

I am more sensitive to other people's needs and I found out that I can relate and connect better and faster with them. I discovered that my mind is one of a solver.

When people tell me or report their problems, I tend to see solutions, ways out, and hopeful endings instead of dead ends, problems, and pessimistic ways of thinking, which I did a lot in the past.

I do care a lot

What people think and take home after they talk with me is mostly that I have no emotions like the Spock character in the very successful series and movies "Star Trek". In reality, I do care and I do have deep feelings about other people's situations and problems, which is why I want to help them solve their problems. For me, that means I care and I can see their problematic situation they are facing from their point of view. If I was like Spock, who, even in the movie, was not a cold person devoid from emotions. Let's not forget that his mother was human (yes, I am a Trekkie). It was just the exterior he had to uphold because of Vulcan culture and etiquette demanded it of him. I wouldn't help them at all if I didn't have even a glimpse of caring emotion in me. People who care help people. People who are indifferent to other people's feelings are not helpful at all. That's my perspective anyway.

Sometimes you need to just shut up and listen.

The area I really fail at a lot, well, let's say had a bit of difficulty at first, is that sometimes, people, and especially women, do not want to get solutions to their problems but want you to just shut up and listen to them, be their friend, a safe ear and shoulder they can lean on, someone who they can unload their everyday worries on, or be a an emotional empty vessel for them to pour their over powering emotions and feelings into.

That's why every time my ex-wife was talking with me and she was throwing problems at my face, I didn't know exactly how to respond. To be a solver, be a man, think like a guy, or just be a listener, be a woman, act like a girl.

Guys, in the future, to avoid any "dangerous" situations like this, before your woman starts her verbal "diarrhea", ask her, in a very polite and casual way, "Do you want me to listen to you as a man and provide solutions or you want me to just listen to what you have to say and be generally quiet and comforting?" I guarantee that will save you from a lot of troubles and will make your girl feel closer to you for even thinking like that in the first place.

New Endeavors.

I started my blog about a year ago without really knowing what I was doing, I did read a lot of books on how to blog and even more articles, but if you don't really try it yourself and see firsthand what works and what doesn't, it is a bit difficult to relate with the books or the articles you read before you start applying what they say.

Let me give you an example. I read in the amazing book about blogging, *How To Blog For Profit: Without Selling Your Soul,* by Ruth Soukup, that using Pinterest as a way to promote your blog is very efficient and gives results.

When I first read the book about 2 years ago, I didn't really take the Pinterest suggestion very seriously. Why didn't I? I thought a bunch of pictures were unable to help me with my blog. I was under the impression that just writing amazing content, content that people will find interesting, informative, and helpful, would be enough to bring people to my blog.

Amazing Content is a must.

It is true, amazing and awesome content is a very important item if you want to have a successful blog but how you present it and also the beautification of the articles with pictures, infographics, and videos is also important. Sometimes, in this visual society we live in with all these new social media services that pop up every 6 months, it is even more important. How you use colors and combinations of colors also play a crucial part in the whole presentation of your blog.

Ruth was right, of course, and it does say that amazing content is king but she also strongly suggests that we use Pinterest as a way to promote and advertise.

Now why did I tell you this story? I told you this story to show you that 2 years ago, I had a specific mindset about services like Pinterest. I thought they were just a bunch of people sharing photos with each other, nothing more, nothing less, which, in its basic form, it is.

Practicality helped me understand.

After I started working on my site and building it and really taking every small consideration in mind that would help with the promotions and increasing the availability and exposure of my site, I realized how powerful images and multimedia are. I noticed that when I beautify my articles with videos, photos, and other media related items, my articles got more exposure and more people started to read them!

Like the Chinese say, a picture is worth a thousand words, or something like that.

The reason I didn't consider that multimedia are so important until quite recently is because I grew up in a house with a father who had a book library full of books with very minimal icons and pictures inside them.

Words are king in my book.

It was, and still is, the words that excite my imagination and take me to worlds and places that are not real, or are real but out of my physical reach.

When I read about Africa and about the Zulus, can hear the thundering steps of large herd of elephants, I can hear the cries of the baby elephants running behind and under their mothers when danger is near.

I can hear the chilling roar of a male lion when he wants to subdue a lioness or scare away other enemies like hyenas or leopards.

I can hear and see in my imaginative eye the Zulus dancing around a big fire, celebrating their kill. I can see the satisfaction in their faces that their efforts were fruitful and that all their stomachs would be full tonight because they brought down a big boar, which is now being cooked over the fire they are dancing around.

I can see mothers breastfeeding their kids, fathers sitting around telling stories to their sons, and elders sharing their wisdom with the younger generation.

I can hear, smell, and taste all these images in my head because they are word generated images. A great writer is the one who uses only words to construct images that are so powerful that the reader feels like he or she was actually there. Over the course of 2 years, my mindset changed completely. Instead of considering multimedia useless because of the way I was raised and the way I was thinking, I was using them every day and trying to describe my articles with images as much as possible.

Complete reversal of point of view.

There was a complete reversal of my way of thinking. How did that happen? How did I manage to do that to myself? The answer is not simple. It is complex and complicated but guess what? All complicated and complex items of this world are made of simpler parts.

Let's take the human body as an example. Looking at it from outside, it looks like it's one entity, and yes, it is. From that specific point of view, our body is one simple entity.

It's when we start doing biology at school or at college or reading books about human anatomy that a sense of panic and chaos takes over us and a sense of awe at the amazing complexity of it.

The vast number of different systems that have to work together in a harmonic synergy to function in the optimum way is breathtaking.

Why do we do things the way we do?

I often ask myself why we do the things we do? and why do we do them with the way we do them?

Do we do them because that's how our parents showed us? Do we do them because that's how our teachers at school taught us?

Do we do them because that's the only way we can do them? Because a friend told us to do it this way?

All the statements above are true. We do things in a specific way because something or someone showed us how. How many of us are doing things the way we want to and not because someone else told us how?

How many of us dare to judge, criticize, and question how things are done? In a family, in a bigger social situation like in a village, an even bigger place like a city, or even a bigger one like a country.

My toothpaste.

Until recently, before I got married, I was using a regular fluoride toothpaste to clean my teeth. To tell you the truth, I wasn't brushing my teeth that often because I am one of the lucky ones. I have genetically strong teeth, I got my father's teeth.

My siblings, namely my brother and sister, who religiously clean and brush their teeth every day, have bad teeth. They have had a number of fillings beginning in childhood.

I know a lot of you out there hate my guts right now, hearing the dentist wheal is not something to joke about.

My ex-wife pointed out that fluoride was not good for our health. Her suggestion was not something that made me angry or created any discomfort. It was something that registered to me as something I needed to research more.

I mean, I was a plant-based eater for the last 2 years. I first stopped eating animal products for my health so hearing my ex-wife suggesting it is better to change my toothpaste to fluoride free was not something I completely rejected.

7

What pissed me off.

The thing that really bothered me was the fact that I hadn't even thought that I could be poisoning myself with other ways except food. The though completely eluded me. If my ex-wife never pointed it out to me, I would still be using fluoride toothpaste.

So what made me change my mindset in this occasion? Was it the calm way and the fact that my ex-wife gave me information that supported her claims and also gave me an alternative?

Was it the fact that I was so much in love with her that if she told me that eating charcoal was good for me, I would do that, too, just to please her?

Was it a combination of my being more open to dietary changes for the last years that enabled me to be open to other changes like health product uses? It's an interesting subject of how the human brain works as far as everyday interactions is concerned. The small interactions like washing your teeth, using a certain soap, wasting water or not, cooking with a specific way, and so many other everyday things we do, subconsciously most of the time, but accumulated together, define our way of living and how we will behave in the present and future!

More changes.

Another thing that I also changed because of my ex-wife was the fact I was using a petroleum-based cream to apply on my nipples and everywhere on my body when there is friction during running, namely under my arm pits and on my genital area.

I knew it was petroleum-based and I was actually inserting carcinogenic substances in my bloodstream through my skin.

That's another puzzle for me. Why on earth would I use this product? Well, there are a number of reasons. First, my neuron synapses had the information that petroleum is bad and also that there are petroleum based products like Vaseline, but it didn't make the connection that petroleum can have deleterious and toxic effects on my health.

I think this happened for a number of reasons. First, I was ignorant of what petroleum really is in these products. Second, it was cheap and convenient. Third, everyone I knew who were running were using it, too. It was also suggested in a lot of running blogs and sites that you should use Vaseline if you want to avoid bloody nipples. Fourth, and for me, the most important of them all, it was working, it was efficient. I didn't have any bloody nipples anymore.

Now I stopped using them and I replaced them with an organic petroleum-free cream that does the same job, has the same results, and has the added advantage that it smells nice. So after running for 4 to 5 hours, which that's how much I run during a long run when I am training for a 50k, I smell nice and the balsam ingredient it contains heals any minor friction generated redness.

Still have bad habits.

Not all of my ex's recommendations panned out though. She also mentioned that the way I clean my ears using those ear sticks was not good for my ear drums. I tried using handmade toilet paper cleaning sticks that were not going all into the ear and also used gravity to get the water out by shifting my head on the side but I only did that for about a week tops, then I started using the sticks again.

Why did I not stop using them? Mind you, I still use them but I make sure not to insert them too far inside my ear. Why didn't I just stop using them and use gravity and a small piece of toilet paper to gather the excess water in my ears after taking a shower? I mean, it's easy and I don't have to worry damaging my ear drum at all.

I really did a soul search about this because logic says stop using them but instead, I keep doing the exact opposite thing. Why is that? I mean, I consider myself to be a man of logic; now that sounded very Spock-like, I'll give you that.

After serious searching, I remember that when I was very little, about 5 to 6 years old, that our mother would take our head, put it on her lap, and using a handmade ear stick made out of cotton and match sticks, would use that to clean out ears of all three of us. It was like a ritual all four of us did after getting after a bath. The reason I couldn't get rid of the ear sticks is because it reminds me, even subconsciously, of the good moments and how happy I was and felt when my mom was cleaning my ears back then. It turns out the emotional bond is too strong for me to stop something that is not good for me.

The truth is, every time I get out of the shower and I am cleaning my ears with these ear buds, I am always thinking, *When are you going to replace them with something else?* I hope to find something alternative in the near future because I want to think I am a person who strives to always become better in every aspect of my life.

Running Endeavor.

When I first started running in 2010, as I mentioned in my first book, *Thirsty for Health,* and also in my following books, *How to train and finish your first 5k race* and *My Weight Loss Journey: How I lost 44 pounds and never gained them back using a plant based diet*, I started running because of sheer vanity. I saw myself in the mirror one day and for the first time, I realized that the ugly, fat man looking back at me in the mirror with the puffy face and the saggy tits and hanging belly and juicy love handles was *me*!

So I started walking at first, then went through a transitional period of time where I was doing walking and running at the same time, and at some point, when I felt that I got into a decent fitness, I started running and I haven't stopped since.

Why am I telling you this and a lot of you who read my books and my articles probably got bored because you read these stories before. Well, I am telling you this to see another mindset shift that occurred in me.

When I started running, pure vanity was fueling my endeavors to do the miles needed to lose the ugly weight, return to a physique that would be acceptable for me, and then stop running. Back then, I saw running as a way to achieve my goal and then throw it to the garbage after I depleted all the usage out of it.

What I didn't expect to happen was ending up loving running so much that I end up adopting it as a lifestyle. Running for me is like breathing, is like food, it's something that I cannot live without.

In the old days, I would literally force myself to get up my couch or my rocking chair, wear my sport running shoes and gear, and drag myself to the high school track, where, with a lot of psychological effort, I would push myself to do the exercises I had designed in my training plan to do that day.

Now, if I miss a training day, I get literally depressed and I feel physically sick to my stomach. The only other time I had this feeling, and is closest to the feeling I have when I lose a running day, is the way I felt when I didn't smoke for a long time and I had severe nicotine withdrawal issues and this emptiness in my stomach was alarmingly intense.

Repeated actions and good habits.

So what made me change my mind? What were the actions or the thoughts that made me reconsider why running should not be just a way to satisfy a means to an end but to be something that I should enjoy every day for my life for the rest of my natural life on this beautiful green blue world?

Well, the actions I did was to get my fat ass outside the house. That was one. The second one was to go to the high school track and start walking and in my effort to lose weight, I started researching about what kind of exercises I can do to lose weight in shorter period of time and in there, intertwined with running, nutrition started to appear. I caught myself reading more nutritional related articles than running.

It turns out that activities that are good for your health like running and you genuinely want to use them as a mean to stay healthy help your mind and your brain to acquire the necessary lacking tools to start viewing and looking life and especially your everyday life with a different lens.

Before I started running, I had a deep case of depression, low self-esteem and very low self-confidence

A bad case of Depression.

All these negative aspects of my life were imprinted in the physical way I was behaving. If you could see me walk from a distance, you would notice that I was always walking looking down like I lost some coins or something!

At my job, I was lacking initiative and even if I had a good idea to propose, I would hold back in fear that I was going to be ridiculed and laughed at. That's a major issue of very low self-confidence to my abilities to do my job correctly and efficiently, and the truth is, I am very good at my job. I love working with computers, that's why I studied them in the first place.

That was pretty much my emotional and psychological side. Physically speaking, I was not that great either. I stopped smoking a year ago and I managed through eating junk food for a year to gain another 22 pounds! So when I started running, I was really in bad shape as far as my body was concerned.

I had still hemorrhoids that were killing me, constipation was still there, and heartburn were still there. The only thing that was not bothering me a lot was my stomach ulcer.

My triglyceride levels were off the charts, I had a mild high blood pressure, and my cholesterol level was near red over 200mg!

The most important of all was the fact that my heart was beating at a rest state at 85 beats per minutes. I had a slight tachycardia. The normal range is 60 to 80 beats per minutes.

So, basically, before I started running, I was a psychologically and physiologically a big mess! Running did save my life as I describe in one of my permanently free books, *How Running Saved My life*.

What did changed my mindset in this case?

So, closing on how I made this mindset switch, I will have to say, except vanity and the pursuit of knowledge, I think seeing firsthand what it did to me, how it transformed me into a better man, both emotionally and psychologically, was one of the many reasons my way of thinking changed. I think having solid results was the one item from the list that pushed me to go exploring even more.

Being lonely is not only a physical situation. There are a lot of people who are physically alone. They live in their one bedroom apartments but have an intense and wild social life, they have friends and buddies and are surrounded by a plethora of other people in their lives. You sure can't called them lonely.

On the other hand, there are so many people out there who have a lot of "friends", acquaintances, and an army of followers and "buddies", but if you look deep into their eyes and basically look even deeper into their soul, you will see sadness and sorrow.

For a long time, I was both! I was living alone, yes, I had a lot of "friends" but my eyes were hollow, unsatisfied, tired. I gave up on life, I was feeling alone, and I was filling those voids with addictions.

Introvert, book reading and going with the flow.

I was very introverted since childhood. Our parents protected us from the outside world, did not allow us to go outside the house often, so my social skills as being around people did not fully develop. Instead, I became a book worm and I was learning through the books how the world was instead of learning it through my interactions with other people.

Everything has its advantage and disadvantages. Books gave me a sense that I can learn everything from them and also gave me a false sense that everything in books must be right. I mean, who would write a book that had errors or didn't want to help people, right? Well, the thought of a 13 year old, which carried me until I was twenty something, that's when I realized the world is not made like most of the books I read but a much, much different story.

I would spend a lot of time in front of my computer, wasting time on online adventures that offered me nothing but meaningless temporary pleasure, online games and online chats, a complete waste of time.

I would eat and drink comfort junk food I would fill my stomach with empty calories while giving myself a temporary spike of sugar rush and a temporary period of pleasurable time, one that I had to repeat many times during the day just to lift my mood up.

That is a dark picture I draw for myself but it was truth for a long period of time. For almost 10 years of my life, I basically didn't know what I was doing. I didn't have any goals or any plans to accomplish, I was going with the flow. I was doing what society was expecting from me, I was eating and drinking what my culture demanded out of me and behaving in stereotype molds that were shaping me me into a robot, into an automatic entity. Basically, I was a human robot or a robot with flesh and blood.

I didn't question anything. I believed what everyone was saying. I was shy and gullible. I was smoking because I thought it made me look cool, which I wasn't as you can clearly see in one of my books, *16 Common Smoking Rationalizations, Recognized, Analyzed, and Ultimately Destroyed!*

I was eating junk food because I didn't want to cook or didn't know how to cook and because I thought back then that eating meat was good for my health.

I was drinking heavily caffeinated soda drinks and lots of coffees, which kept me in a situation of chronic stress.

I would think too much of what other people were doing instead of concentrating on accomplishing my own goals I would compare my life's progress with other people around me like comparing my life with other people's lives is something that you will ever derive any useful conclusions.

Every person is unique, we are like snowflakes, like I say often in my books. I like to use this analogy because everyone understands what I want to convey.

Running Transformation.

My engagement with running made me transform from a depressed individual into a happy person. Now, when I walk down the street, my head is not looking down at the ground but in front of me and sometimes a little bit higher to the sky! I don't have thoughts of bad situations, sad scenarios, or what if's or wishful thinking. Now my thoughts are happy, positive, I see the good in bad, and managed, with the help of running and other aids, to transform myself into an extrovert. Now I am not as shy as I used to be. I want to go out more often, I want to meet new people and make new acquaintances and make more friends, and I especially love meeting people who share the same passion as I have with running.

What made me change from an introvert to an extrovert? What made me get rid of my depression and what made me change from a pessimist to an optimist?

I think the important item that made me see the light so to speak was the repeated actions that running offers. You need to do certain actions over and over again, increasing the quality and quantity of them gradually, and in time, you will start to see tangible results. I think it's the physical metamorphosis that you can see with your own eyes that then helps you change your mindset and a new inner, emotional, and psychological metamorphosis happens, which then will support and drive your current condition and transform it into a lifestyle!

After running for 6 months and successfully losing about 14 to 16 kilos, that's 30 to 35 pounds approximately for my American friends, I reached a stalemate as losing weight.

It didn't matter if I ran a half-marathon every day, 7 days a week, nonstop, I wasn't losing a gram.

Don't put your eggs in one basket.

At first, I got disappointed and I got disappointed because I put all my eggs in one basket, namely running. I assumed that just by running, I would be able to shed all the fat off my body.

I was very sad and angry with myself for a long time because in my mind, I had hit a dead end!

Then I met with some vegan athletes when I entered to run 217 km! Yes, I know that did not end well but that's another story for another book and article, and they suggested to me that nutrition plays a paramount role in athletic performance, especially vegetarian nutrition programs.

I must admit the thought that food played any role in my running performance yet along losing weight was something that I rejected from the start as hocus pocus. I am sure there are a lot of people out there today who have the same mindset as I had 4 years ago, that food is irrelevant with our health and doesn't play any role what so ever.

Evil Medical Establishment.

That's what the medical establishment, especially in the so called Western societies, like the USA, UK, EU, Canada, and Australia, to name a few. Doctors in these countries think that someone gets sick because of a virus or a bug or because of heritage, namely DNA, because that's how they were taught in their medical colleges and universities.

They are under the false impression that drugs and medicine are the solution to all illnesses and diseases. They are trained to manage the symptoms, not to heal and treat the cause.

Let me give you an example. People with type 2 diabetes are told to stay away from fruits and vegetables because they are full of "sugar" and will make their condition even worse. Type 2 diabetes is the condition where the body creates enough insulin, but cannot take the sugar from the blood or it doesn't take enough out of the blood stream, ending up with the sugar building up in the blood. As a result, the sugar is trapped there.

This creates a range of medical problems like possible blindness, and the smallest wound on you can turn into gangrene and you may lose an arm or a leg!

So they give people drugs to regulate their sugar, which they are fine if you want to incorporate more side effects from drugs in your life.

The cure for Type 2 diabetes has been known for some years now. It's a whole plant-based diet, yes, a vegan diet. The reason insulin cannot remove the excess sugar from our blood is because the inner layer of the arteries are clogged and filled with fat, which prevents the transportation of sugar into the cells and out of your blood stream.

What doctors should tell Type 2 diabetic patients is to not stop eating fruits and vegetables but to stop consuming foods that are high in saturated fats and cholesterol, namely, meat, dairy products, seafood, fish, and processed and refined carbohydrates. They should be told to stay away from any kind of oils whether animal- or plant-based.

I don't want you to believe me, I want you to search and question as far as Type 2 diabetes is concerned. Check out this amazing book written by Dr. Neal Barnard.

No dead ends.

I mentioned all these to see that there are no dead ends, there is only ignorance, nothing more and nothing less. I was an ignorant person as far as nutrition is concerned.

The fact that I did not give up running and continue pursuing it, trying to make better personal records and losing the sick weight was the vessel that allowed me to experiment with nutrition.

If running was not in the picture for me to prick my mind to challenge me to go forward with this, I don't think I would have ever considered nutrition. I would still be fat, and still eating junk food because I would still think that food doesn't have anything to do with the way I look or how healthy or unhealthy I am!

Mind blowing nutrition.

When I found nutrition, my mind was blown away in such proportion that, at first, I was so overwhelmed from the information I didn't know existed because let's face it I was an ignorant little man. For a few days, I just stopped reading and acquiring new data to give my brain the time to create the new neural paths an time to process it. I know the thing I am going to say will sound crazy but I am going to say it anyway. I think, I think I could actually feel and hear the new neural pathways being created, I could literally feel my brain expanding!

It was there, in black and white, a whole new world for me to explore, nutrition and its direct or indirect effects on my athletic performance and possible weight loss options.

I was 78 kilos (171 pounds) and I wanted to lose another 6 kilos (13 pounds) to be in my BMI health zone. BMI is Body Mass Index and it's an index that gives you an estimate of how healthy you are based on your height and weight using a very simple mathematical equation.

Eliminating the bad food.

The first thing I started removing from my diet was refined and processed carbohydrates. Like sweets made out from white sugar, I also stopped eating bread made out of white flour, and sodas namely sweet ice teas packed with artificial colorings and sugar.

I did that and continued with my training program as usual and by the end of one month, I lost 2 kilos (4.4 pounds)

Then more research came into play and I started removing fried food from my diet, like fried potatoes, which allowed me to lose another 2 kilos (4.4 pounds) in a month.

I was down to 74 kilos (162 pounds). I forgot to tell you that I am 1.74cm tall, that's about 5'9" so I was okay now, normal for my height!

I could have easily stopped running now because I achieved my goal but that was the thought I had 2 years ago. I had learned so much about nutrition and so much about running that I knew to my core that to maintain a healthy weight, running and my new dietary regime had to become a lifestyle, otherwise I would just end up going back to junk food and ending up being a couch potato again!

I decided to experiment even more with this nutrition and I stop eating butter and eggs and I completely removed olive oil from my diet. A few months later, and I had lost 4 kilos (8.8 pounds)!

It didn't take long to figure out what made me fat. You get fat if you eat fat, especially saturated fat, the kind of fat that is in all animals.

 After experimenting with nutrition and keeping my running training program pretty much the same, I decided that eating meat, fish, dairy products, and seafood was not offering me anything I couldn't get from plants. On the contrary, they were giving me substances that would make me sick in the future with diseases like cardiac diseases, stroke, Type 2 diabetes, kidney stones, and some types of cancer like colorectal cancer. The list is long!

May of 2013, a year after experimenting, I officially went to an only plant-based diet and I am still applying this lifestyle in nutrition today and it's something that I am sure to my core I will be doing until I die.

I continued experimenting with different plant-based food and at some point, I managed to get down to 67 kilos (148 pounds) but that was too thin for me so now I am between 70 to 72 kilos (154 to 158 pounds) and I feel fantastic.

What made the mind switch possible.

Now what made me change my mindset? I'm afraid knowledge on its own was not enough. I think it's the application of knowledge. The practical applications of theories are the ones that provide us with results and feedback that later we use, act upon, and make decisions.

I saw firsthand that if I adopt a <u>diet rich in plants</u> and eliminate the animal products as much as I can I saw tangible results. I lost a number of pounds in stages as I described earlier by excluding animal fat and refined products and increasing my whole plant intake to maintain the balance in calories and in nutritional elements like vitamins, minerals, antioxidants, and so on.

I saw results and I was convinced that this kind of lifestyle is good for me, is healthy for me, and when someone doesn't have problems with his/her health, that's when he or she is truly happy.

Where all started.

All the stories I just shared with you would never have happened if something really amazing had not happened to me in April of 2009. After being a heavy smoker of cigarettes for 16 years, I realized that <u>smoking was killing me</u>, doh! I know how stupid it sounds now. I am 7 years smoke free and going strong and celebrating every April like it's my birthday because that's the day I literally was reborn.

For me, smoking was a big part of my life and it really messed me up in more ways than usual. Aside from the physiological damage to the body, nicotine shrinks our arteries, making us more prone to heart diseases like heart attack and stroke. The carbon monoxide poisons our brain by limiting the amount of oxygen delivered to our brain and to the rest of our body. The 4,000 chemicals that are inhaled with every cigarette end up sitting and accumulating on our lungs are the parts that make up tar. 60 to 90 of them are scientifically proven to be carcinogenic and they are rotting and destroying our lungs' ability to get oxygen!

There are some of the effects smoking does to our health but we continue smoking with a vengeance, thinking that it will not happen to us, that cancer and other smoking related illnesses and diseases happen only to other people not us. That's a dangerous mindset to have and that's a mindset I had for many years.

Drug addict years.

I was smoking because I thought it was cool. I was smoking because I thought it made me look more smart and sophisticated, I smoked because I thought it made me look manlier and a lot of other stupid excuses and ignorant hypothesis!

Most smokers die from nicotine effects, not tar effects. Most smokers don't die from lung or esophageal cancer. Someone must smoke for a number of years to get these kind of cancers must smoke.

It's nicotine that gets you first. Nicotine is one of the most highly powerful alkaloid substances on the planet.

You only need one puff to get hooked and addicted, just one small puff. It's not a habit, smoking cigarettes is not a habit. I repeated this information in my book, *16 Common Smoking Rationalizations, Recognized, Analyzed, and Ultimately Destroyed!*

A habit requires repetition for three to four weeks. Let's say a physiological need, for your body to crave it. Nicotine created addiction as soon as it gets to the body and especially the brain. It takes over your brain and enslaves you into a lifetime of prison that will take your health away, your hard earned dollars, and will leave you with nothing to show at the end of the road!

This is not the worst of smoking though. Yes, you read right! The health issues and the fact that you lose a fortune buying them are not what should worry you. It's the psychological association you do that you cannot live without smoking! When you spend a lifetime smoking, you associate everything with the act of smoking.

Deadly associations.

You drink your <u>coffee</u> and you smoke, you eat and after you eat, you smoke, you have sex and you smoke after.

The phone rings and because you don't want to take the chance to be left without your fix in case the phone call goes for a long time, you smoke. When you are using the toilet, you smoke!

You smoke before go into the cinema, you smoke when there is intermission. You smoke, smoke, smoke your life away and subconsciously, <u>you relate everything with smoking.</u>

False stress management with smoking.

You even think you manage stress with smoking. In reality, that's not true. Stress and smoking have nothing in common except one thing.

When you stress, or when you drink alcohol or when you get mega doses of <u>vitamin C</u>, more than 10mg, your urine becomes acidic, more than usual. The body, being this beautiful and all wise machine, takes the first alkaloid available in the blood, which, in the non-smoker's case, is calcium either from dietary intake or from the bones. In the smoker's case, it takes nicotine and dumps it into the urine so it will make the urine alkaline.

When this happens, the smoker starts to feel the effects of drug withdrawal, nicotine withdrawal, so he goes for his cigarettes.

He or she thinks that smoking is relieving stress but in reality, he just feeds his addiction. Stress relief or management has nothing to do with smoking, it's a false association because of a lack of basic knowledge of what stress does to you and smokers think they manage stress.

Psychological Cravings.

When I was a smoker, obviously I did not know this information. I know these things because even after 7 years of non-smoking, I still catch myself wanting a cigarette and I want to understand why. Well, I found out why. It's the psychological association I did that I cannot live without a cigarette and when I sometimes catch myself wanting one it is because a social event happened and for the first time, I am called to deal with it without using a cigarette. That's the reason, the physiological addiction is gone, nicotine leaves your body the first 3 days in huge quantities and in 2 weeks, it's gone from your system.

What made me change the way I was thinking about smoking and made me realized that I was killing myself was an incident where it made me scared that I would not be able to have the life I always dreamed I would have. When I got scared that my quality of life will be downgraded and would lose my life, that's when it kicked in.

The realization for people who quit smoking successfully are as many as the people themselves. The way to quit smoking and have a high rate for success for me is only one method available: *go cold turkey.* Any other method will only make you suffer more, prolong the withdrawal period, and most of the time, you will go back to smoking.

I promise I will have more about this in an upcoming book, where I will present a complete method of how to successfully quit smoking using the *cold turkey method.*

So what changed my mindset that lead me to stop smoking? In this case, it was fear, plain and simple genuine fear of losing something that I consider very valuable, life, and most important the ability to create life, namely be able to find a good woman that wants the same things as me and creating a healthy and happy family. If I continued smoking, I don't think I would be here alive today talking to you.

Conclusion.

I hope that my stories helped you think, question, evaluate, and reevaluate certain aspects of your life and how you can make them better, how you can start using your head to find ways that will not lead you to dead ends, or pessimistic scenarios for your life, but to start thinking like a doer, like a winner, like a problem solver. I hope my stories made you "wake" up like I did 7 years ago when I stopped smoking, which lead to weight gain, which lead to running, which lead to nutrition and all these areas of my life. *Each time, I had to change my mindset*, otherwise I would be dead by now or suffering from a crippling disease like a heart attack, a stroke, or worse, death.

I always love when a writer recaps their book so here is a cheat list of the article/book. Here is the reasons in a Spartan form that made me personally change my way of thinking.

Reasons That Made Me Change My Way of Thinking in Different Time Periods

1. *A loved one approach made me reconsider a few things. The way you will present your arguments plays a big role and I think a loved one, either a spouse, girlfriend, wife, or other family member have a higher chance of getting through you.*
2. *Emotional attachment is very strong, especially if items and people are involved from childhood. The key is to use your logic and hard scientific evidence as your compass when you are called to make a decision.*

3. *Exercise and repeated acts following a plan helps the brain to create the necessary pathways that will enable us to put the theory into action.*
4. *Search and research should never be put on hold because we think we have learned everything. We must criticize and judge and evaluate our current knowledge constantly; nothing is constant, everything is floating.*
5. *Finally, strong emotions like fear could trigger mindset changes.*

Have a healthy and happy day.

My warmest regards,

Andreas Michaelides

Other books by Andreas Michaelides

Thirsty For Health

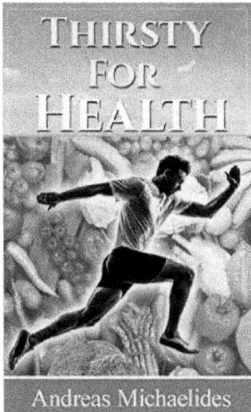

A truly eye opening book that should and will make your question yourself and everything you have done so far diet and lifestyle wise. Obesity, caffeine and junk food addiction, smoking and digestive problems? This is the place you can start answering your most asked questions. A book you wish you had found earlier, an amazing story that had to be told in order to help others not to go through the same misery. In these pages you will learn how to regain control over your life, how to find strength from within in order to go through life's numerous challenges, successfully overcome addictions and finally tune in to genuine health and happiness. You are the alchemist, the architect of your life and no one else but you have the power to make the change. Be the change that you want to see in the world. You can start now and this book will help you do that and more and you will also learn how to live long and live well.

The Food I Grew Up With...Veganized!

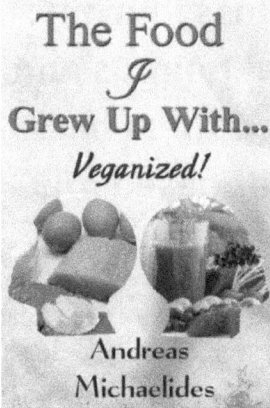

I wrote this book first to thank my mother for never letting me without food on the table and secondly to show to people out there that they can thrive on a plant based diet and the most important of all they don't have to start from zero as food is concerned I hope I will show with this book that you can transform many of your old food into new versions of plant based ones. This book is not a

27

cookbook although it contains a lot of the food recipes I used to and still eating today. All the recipes are a result of many interviews with my mother which without her this book would never be possible. This book basically shows one aspect of my psyche as food is concerned and how I deal with it transitioning from an omnivore to a herbivore.

How to train and finish your first 5k race.

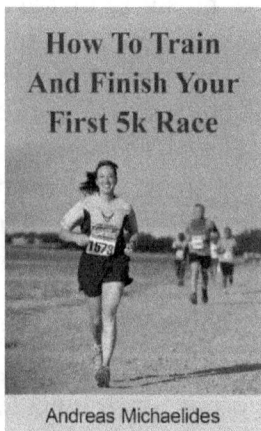

How To Train And Finish Your First 5k Race

Andreas Michaelides

You can watch other people running on the TV, playing football, basketball, or baseball. At least those guys are getting paid to run and jump and tackle. Why should you go through this torture of actually getting up from your soft chair and making yourself go through this ordeal? Why would you enter this nightmare? Why not continue your ignorant bliss of a lovely sedentary life where all you need to do is push the buttons of a remote control and then people in the box can live your desires, your fantasies, your dreams, and ultimately, your life?

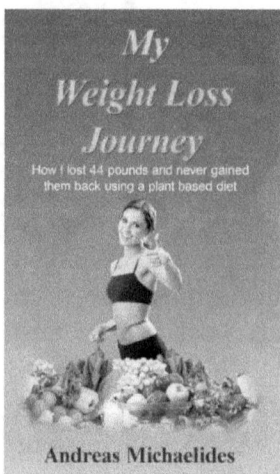

My Weight Loss Journey
How I lost 44 pounds and never gained them back using a plant based diet

Andreas Michaelides

My weight loss journey: How I lost 44 pounds and never gained them back using a plant based diet

Although I never expected to drag myself out of the house and go for a run, after I finished those first three rounds at the high school track in my village, everything changed. I was so exhausted—which was an indicator of how lacking my physical fitness was—but after all the discomfort, itching, and rash in various places due to friction from excess fat, for the first time, I felt renewed, and memories of running and coming in first place in high school reminded me of how I used to be compared to how I was after those three laps around the track.

It made my eyes water; I was alone in the middle of the track under an April sky full of stars when tears of mixed feelings started pouring down from my eyes. Emotionally and psychologically, it was a turning point for me, and it also made me even more determined to become that lean, mean running machine I used to be. It was right there in that single moment that I saw the path I had to follow.

16 Common Smoking Rationalizations Recognized, Analyzed And Ultimate Destroyed.

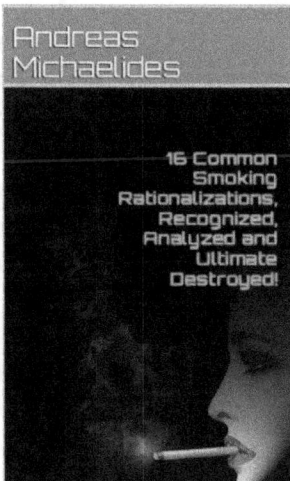

Andreas Michaelides

16 Common Smoking Rationalizations, Recognized, Analyzed and Ultimate Destroyed!

So my fellow people, non-smokers, ex-smokers, and current smokers, let's begin the catharsis, let's learn a few useful truths of what smoking is, what nicotine is, and arm ourselves with some solid truthful, factual arguments to use. The non-smokers and ex-smokers can use them when they talk with other smokers and for the smokers to help them come to that realization point that you are a drug addict, and you need to recover to your previous nicotine free state, because trust me, that state is where you will find your true

42 Weight Loss Tips, That Will Change Your Life Forever

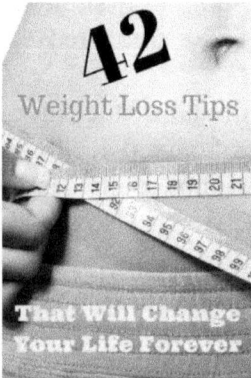

Andreas Michaelides

What made me get off my fat ass was vanity, yes I admit it, I didn't start losing weight because I wanted to be healthy or because it was the right thing to do; no, it was straightforward and pure vanity. I wanted to return to that lean, mean, fit, sexy running machine I used to be in high school.

Well, if you read thus far, it means you already started to change your way of thinking, so let's start losing those pounds safely and healthy, and never gain them back.

Please write a review.

I consider myself as a person that wants to think that I am constantly improving my books, my work and myself. I am always trying to deliver to my readers the best quality and current information out there as my area of interest and expertise is concern which is Health, Nutrition and Exercise.

In order to accomplish that I need feedback from you and the only feedback I know that will help me achieve a relative perfection in all areas of my life is your valuable reviews so I know where I am wrong or where I have made mistakes and errors.

There is no such thing as a perfect book out there, perfection for one person is a sloppy work for other, so in order to satisfy as much as people out there my books need to be updated regularly and it doesn't matter if it is in electronic form (kindle) or paperback form.

 If you found this book useful, please leave your review with all your thoughts, don't hold back, it will only take a few minutes of your time.

 If you didn't like this book, please let me know by contacting me and I will give my best shot to fix the issue.

Thank you very much,

My warmest regards

Andreas Michaelides